I0206728

Six-Word Lessons for Raising Conscious Children

100 Lessons Rooted in Confidence, Connection and Trust

Renee Metty

Published by Pacelli Publishing
Bellevue, Washington

SIX ~WORD LESSONS

Six-Word Lessons for Raising Conscious Children

Cover and interior designed by Pacelli Publishing
Cover photo by Felix Montino, Flickr, licensing by CreativeCommons.org
Author photo by Kim Beer

Published by Pacelli Publishing
9905 Lake Washington Blvd. NE, #D-103
Bellevue, Washington 98004
PacelliPublishing.com

ISBN 10: 1-967256-02-0
ISBN-13: 978-1-967256-02-0

Dedication

To Noah, Cain, and Selah—

You have been my deepest calling and my greatest teachers.

You are the rhythm my life flows to.

Thank you for letting me grow beside you and for shaping me. Thank you for teaching me what presence really means.

You are the reason this exists.

This book was written in the in-between moments— a reflection of our journey.

May you always trust your essence, and remember that presence is the most powerful thing you can ever offer.

To Rusty—

For holding space for all of us to become and allowing space for your own becoming.

For the parents doing the inner work *while raising the next generation.—*

May this book remind you that presence is enough, connection is powerful, and the small moments always mattered most.

And to every parent who's ever wondered, "Am I doing this right?" This is your reminder:

You're already doing something extraordinary..

Contents

Introduction

We live in a world that celebrates performance, productivity, and perfectly filtered parenting. But raising a human isn't about checking boxes—it's about connection and building a relationship that lasts.

Raising children is a gift not to be taken lightly and yet not too seriously. Parenting is not to follow rules or to have the perfect strategy. It is not about compliance or performance. Parenting is about showing up in the imperfect moment and choosing connection anyway. We're raising humans to remember who they are. And to do that, we must remember who *we* are too. Hopefully, with the following lessons, you remember sooner than I did.

This book was born from years of listening: to children, to parents, to my own body, to the quiet truths that rise in the everyday. This was born from remembering and becoming—from my own experience as a parent, educator, and entrepreneur. This book is not a blueprint. It's a companion. You won't find perfection here—only presence, perspective, and practical steps that support both your child *and* your growth as a parent.

It's for the parent who wants to raise confident, kind, resilient humans—*without losing themselves in the process.* It's a blend of practice and pause, intuition and integration.

Parenting can be noisy. But underneath the logistics and pressure and to-dos, there is a frequency worth tuning into. That's what this book invites: a chance to slow down and listen. To the child in front of you. To the child inside of you. To your own sacred knowing.

You'll see whispers of **The Cove School** and **With Pause** in its rhythm and feel the grounding energy of **Trusting Equus** in its steadiness. This isn't a manual—it's a moment of presence, offered in pages.

I don't trust one-size-fits-all parenting. I trust in presence over perfection. I trust in connection, not control.

I trust in respect over reaction. I trust that every child wants to be seen, not shaped. And I know –

and I don't mean cognitive knowing, but that deep felt sense of knowing—that parenting is one of the most sacred invitations we'll ever receive.

Inside, you'll find 100 six-word lessons organized by theme, each with a short reflection and an actionable step. You can read it cover to cover or flip to the section you need in the moment. There's no right way to use this book—only your way. You'll notice the chapters are short. The lessons are simple. That's on purpose. Each six-word title anchors a deeper truth, and each reflection is designed to reconnect you with your instincts—not override them.

These aren't quick fixes. They're invitations. To pause. To notice. To connect. Because what you model now becomes your child's inner compass later. And the most powerful tool you have in parenting? You. Regulated, rooted, and real.

If you're looking for perfection, you won't find it here. But if you're looking for permission to pause, breathe, and choose presence—tune on in.

Wherever you are on your parenting path, you're welcome here. You're right on time.

Deepen Bonds through Everyday Small Moments

1

Speak less, listen more, connect deeply.

In our fast-paced world, it's easy to fall into the trap of speaking more than we listen. But deep connection is built on listening and hearing. It's built in the silence between the words. When we quiet ourselves and tune into our child's world, we send a message that their voice matters. Create "listening moments" each day where you simply listen, without distractions, to your child's thoughts, feelings, or observations.

Be eye level, engage with presence.

We often stand above our little ones, physically and emotionally. Yet, when we get on their level, we show them respect and connect more deeply. This simple shift changes the dynamic from authority to partnership. Kneel or sit next to them when offering direction or support. It invites cooperation over compliance. Notice how the energy shifts when your presence feels less like a command and more like an invitation.

3

Narrate life—language that sparks curiosity.

Your voice is their first tour guide. Narrating what you're doing or noticing builds vocabulary and models how to move through the world with curiosity. "I see a red leaf falling" might become their internal voice of wonder. Pick one routine—like snack time or getting dressed—and narrate it gently, like you're telling a story together. Simple words unlock a richer understanding of their surroundings. Ask them questions that invite exploration.

Hold space, let feelings move through.

Children don't yet have the tools to process intense feelings alone. Big emotions are not a problem to fix—they're energy to be witnessed. Holding space means not rushing, not solving, only being. When we hold space, we're offering containment without control. They borrow our nervous systems to learn regulation. During a meltdown, pause. Breathe. Say, "I'm here with you," and wait. No need to rush the wave—ride it together.

5

Play is conversation, join their world.

Play isn't a break from learning—it *is* the learning. It's how your child communicates what they care about, what they're working through, and how they make sense of life. When you enter their play, you're stepping into relationship. You're saying, "I see you." For ten minutes, let them lead the play, and follow along—no teaching, no correcting, only curiosity. Let their story unfold and allow them to be the guide.

Snuggles now, security later, trust grows.

You're not only offering warmth—you're building their inner sense of "I am loved." Affection in the early years isn't spoiling—it's scaffolding. You're wiring in security that supports independence later. That security becomes the foundation they stand on for life. Add affection to transitions—after waking, before leaving, or before bed. A snuggle, a kiss, or hug can become anchoring rituals that build trust and ease. Physical connection lowers stress. No words needed.

7

Laughter bonds; repair happens through joy.

Joy is a powerful reset button. When things feel off, a moment of shared laughter can bring you back to each other. Laughter doesn't ignore the hard—it lightens and repairs it. It is a fast track to reconnection as it melts stress and softens resistance. Create a "go-to giggle ritual"—a song, a game, a voice—something silly that's yours. Humor disarms without dismissing. Use it when things feel disconnected or heavy.

Validate emotions, don't rush to fix.

When your child's upset, your instinct might be to soothe it away. Children aren't asking us to remove discomfort, they're asking us to be with them in it. Validation teaches that emotions are welcome—not problems to erase. Practice naming the feeling aloud without judgment: "You're feeling mad because your block tower fell," before offering any redirection. Let your child feel fully felt before moving on. No need to explain it away.

9

Show up fully, devices down first.

Children can tell when our attention is divided. And over time, they internalize that divided attention as disconnection. Presence is your most powerful form of love. Even a short moment of undivided attention builds more connection than hours of half-presence. Create daily "tech-free touchpoints" (like snack time or bath). Ten minutes of eye contact and presence tells your child, "You matter!"

Love them first, teach them second.

Discipline without connection feels like rejection. When you lead with love, your child is more open to guidance. Love is not a reward for "good" behavior—it's the foundation from which all learning can happen. Without connection, teaching falls flat. When a behavior triggers you or you feel tempted to jump into fixing, teaching, or redirecting, pause and offer warmth first. Ask yourself: "Have I connected before correcting?"

Emotional Regulation Begins With Your Example

11

Your regulated nervous system guides theirs.

Your child borrows your nervous system until they develop their own regulation tools. They feel you more than they hear you. Regulation isn't only for you—it's contagious. Regulation begins with your response, not their behavior. You are the thermostat, not the thermometer. Your calm resets the room. Create a grounding cue—a hand on your heart, a breath, a mantra like "slow is strong." Use it before addressing any big emotions.

Start with neutral; build from connection.

Neutral doesn't mean cold—it means grounded. We often come in hot—correcting, scolding, or fixing. Yet, children respond best when we meet them with neutrality, not reactivity. Meeting your child with connection before correction makes learning possible. Approach tough moments like a scientist: curious, not furious. Before responding, check in with, "Am I connected or correcting?" Pause. Then lead with warmth.

13

Regulate yourself first, regulated child follows.

You can't coach calm from chaos. Your ability to regulate yourself shapes how your child learns to handle their world. When you steady your own system, you give your child something solid to attune to. Build a "pause practice." Name what you feel in hard moments: "I'm feeling overwhelmed, and I'm taking a breath." Anchor yourself before you guide them. Let them witness the practice in action.

Meltdowns aren't manipulation, they're overwhelmed circuits.

A meltdown isn't defiance or testing boundaries—it's a signal that your child's nervous system is overloaded. They're not intentionally giving you a hard time; they're having one. During a meltdown, shift your lens: "This is communication, not conflict." Your calm presence regulates what their brain can't yet handle. Stay close, stay small and emotionally steady. Save the lesson for later—allow them to express without fear of rejection.

15

Soft eyes, open arms, stay present.

Children read you more than they hear you. Your posture speaks volumes. Soften your eyes, open your arms, lower your tone—these are signals of security your child feels before you ever speak. Your energy matters. Harsh energy escalates. Soft energy co-regulates. When your child is struggling, check your body first. Relax your jaw, drop your shoulders soften your gaze. Presence starts in the body.

Help them name, tame big feelings.

Feelings are overwhelming when they have no name. When you help your child put words to emotions, you're giving them tools for self-awareness and future regulation. It's the first step toward taming the chaos. This language builds a child's emotional literacy and reduces their fear of big internal experiences. Use "I wonder" language: "I wonder if you're feeling mad because your toy broke." Wondering invites connection without pressure to be "right."

17

Self-regulation begins with secure connection.

Before your child can regulate their body or emotions, they need to feel connected. Connection is the access point to calm. Regulation requires trust—and trust begins with connection. It's the doorway to every emotional skill. Build micro-moments of connection throughout the day. A quick cuddle. A knowing look. A shared smile. These moments become the anchors your child regulates from.

Teach "pause" moments, not "stop" commands.

"Stop!" is often our go-to word under stress—but it rarely teaches anything. Guiding your child to pause gives them a tool for self-awareness, not obedience. Stopping is reactive. Pausing is conscious. It creates space between impulse and action, and that space is where growth lives. Create a shared "pause cue"—a word, a hand signal, or even a breath together. Use it during low-stakes moments to build the skill.

19

Prioritize peace, then layer routines gradually.

Peace is the foundation, structure is the scaffold. But peace doesn't mean chaos. It means calm energy first, then intentional routines layered in slowly. Routines only work when your child is regulated enough to follow them. Don't pile structure onto a shaky emotional base. Scan your day to find the resistance. Start there. Can you make that moment peaceful before making it structured? Make connection the first step, not the last.

Be their anchor, not their storm.

You are their home base—the one they turn to when everything feels too much. When your child is spiraling, they don't need you to match the chaos. They need you to hold the ground. Be the calm in their internal storm. Choose an anchor mantra for yourself, perhaps, "I am steady." Whisper it internally when your child is dysregulated—it will change your energy.

Kind but Firm Boundaries Build Security

21

Boundaries guide not punish; stay kind

When boundaries are rooted in kindness, it creates an environment of guidance, openness and acceptance. Punishment triggers defense; guidance fosters growth. It guides children toward responsibility and self-trust. Children need to know where the line is and that you'll walk it with them. When setting a boundary, drop the threat. "I won't let you hit me. I'll stay close while you're upset." Kindness doesn't cancel clarity.

Say “yes” to needs, “no” kindly.

Kindness and boundaries aren’t opposites. You can say “no” to a behavior while still saying “yes” to the underlying need. Kind limits affirm the person even when correcting the action. Saying “no” with empathy teaches children to handle limits with resilience, not rebellion. Practice combining a “yes” to the feeling with a “no” to the behavior. “Yes, you’re frustrated. No, you can’t hit.” Let both truths coexist.

23

Connect first, correct second, stay firm.

Connection is the foundation for all learning, not a reward for good behavior. When children feel disconnected, correction lands as rejection. Connection opens the door to change. When children feel they can express emotion without judgment, they're more open to feedback. Next time you need to redirect, say their name gently, get to eye level, and connect before you correct. Let love lead the boundary.

Calm limits help, harsh words hurt.

Limits are necessary, but delivery matters. Harshness may get short-term compliance, but calm earns long-term trust. A child's nervous system hears your tone more than your words. Harshness triggers fear and shuts down learning. We're not raising obedience—we're raising self-awareness. Practice delivering a limit in your "library voice." Quiet but clear. Calm but confident. It's surprising how well children respond to tone. It shapes the message more than the rule.

25

Be consistent, predictable, and emotionally available.

Consistency is love in action. When you follow through calmly and reliably, your child learns that you are dependable. Children feel secure when they know what to expect. Predictable boundaries paired with emotional availability build security and trust. It's not rigidity—it's reliability. Check your energy, so you can respond, not react. Can you be emotionally present and follow through? Don't only repeat the rule—show up with warmth behind it.

Kindness and firmness work best together.

Firmness without kindness can feel cold. Kindness without firmness feels unstable. When you blend both, your child feels held enough to grow and strong enough to stretch. True leadership in parenting is rooted in both kindness and clarity. Practice “friendly firmness”—soften your face, and keep your words clear: “I hear you. The answer’s still no.” Pair warmth with a firm boundary to model healthy authority.

27

Offer choices; prevent power struggles early.

Power struggles often come from feeling powerless. Children crave a sense of control. Choices allow your child to feel respected, even when they don't get their way. It offers agency without chaos and leads to cooperation more often than commands. It's not giving in—it's guiding with options. Offer moments in your routine where you can offer choice: which shoes to wear or what book to read. Predictable autonomy lowers resistance.

Teach security, not blind obedience rules.

We're not raising rule-followers—we're raising thinkers. Blind obedience trains compliance. Teaching the "why" behind rules builds trust and critical thinking. Help them see boundaries as care, not control. Obedience fades. Understanding lasts. Reframe your language from "Because I said so" to "Here's why this helps you." Connect rules to their real-world function. Even toddlers absorb the message behind the boundary.

29

Follow-through matters more than threats.

Threats escalate power struggles and erode trust. Follow-through builds trust and ends the struggle. Your child doesn't need to fear you—they need to trust your boundaries. Choose one repeating challenge. Replace threat with follow-through. Instead of "If you throw that again," use "Looks like it's hard to use this safely. I'm going to hold onto it." Practice doing it without anger, like you'd zip a coat. Steady action.

Guidelines serve growth, not enforcing control.

Respect over rules. Rules tell children what to do. Guidelines teach them how to be and offer structure without rigidity. They're rooted in values, not control. When we parent through respect, we guide from the inside out—not through fear, but through trust. Swap, "Because I said so" with "In our family, we…" It invites your child into a shared value system, not an obedience loop.

Confidence Grows through Independence and Effort

31

Help me to do it myself.

Independence isn't about pushing them away—it's about believing they're capable. When we jump in too soon, we rob them of the win. Support just enough and then step back. Our job is to scaffold, not solve. Self-trust is beginning to form when they want to do it themselves. Offer the first step: "I'll hold the sleeve; you slide your arm in." Let them take it from there.

Teach skills slowly, step-by-step.

Skill-building isn't a one-time lesson—it's a layered process. What's obvious to you is brand new to them. Patience turns frustration into momentum. When we rush skill-building, we teach overwhelm, not mastery. Teaching step-by-step gives your child a chance to feel capable instead of discouraged. Narrate your steps slowly. Instead of "Let's get dressed," offer: "Let's find your shirt. Then we pull it over your head." Use building blocks of small actionable steps.

33

Small wins today, confidence for life.

Confidence is built through progress and courage. Confidence grows in small, repeatable successes—not big, flashy moments. Model your thought process through challenges and small wins. Each little success wires in self-trust and readiness for more. Celebrate the next small win, not with praise for the result, but curiosity about how they did it: "Wow, how did you figure that out?" Invite your child to reflect on what felt easy and what felt tricky.

Challenges are opportunities; growth follows struggle.

Growth doesn't come from avoiding struggle—it comes from moving through it. Challenges are where learning gets sticky (and powerful). It's the very thing that builds resilience Reframe "failures" as feedback and make them opportunities to grow. The next time your child gets stuck, pause. Ask, "What do you think your options are?" Sit in the moment with them instead of solving.

35

Trust them more, hover over less.

Your trust is their permission slip to commit. When we micromanage every move, we crowd out curiosity and confidence. Hovering sends a subtle message: “I don’t think you can.” Stepping back says, “I trust in you.” Trust creates space for courage. Instead of saying, “Be careful,” offer: “I trust you to figure it out. I’ll be here.” Trust + presence = powerful combo.

Let them experiment, even if messy.

Mess isn't failure—it's practice in progress. Skill-building can be messy by nature. Letting them work through it grows resilience and problem-solving far more than doing it "right." When children are offered the space to experiment, they learn to trust themselves. Set up a "Yes Mess" space using art, water-play or snack prep supplies, and invite your child into a messy experience.Celebrate the effort, not the cleanup.

37

Process matters more than perfect results.

Perfection robs the joy from learning. But process? That's where discovery lives. Guide them to notice how they approached a task—not only how it ended. When we focus on the result, we send the message: "Only outcomes matter." Focusing on the process nurtures curiosity, creativity, and grit. Replace praise. Instead of "Good job," offer "You really kept going, even when it was hard." Highlight their experience, not their execution.

Build responsibility, not fear of failure.

Responsibility isn't about pressure—it's about ownership. When we lead with fear, we create performance anxiety. When we lead with trust, we build capable humans. Fear says: "Careful, you might spill." Responsibility says: "You can do it" or "Your contribution is important." The difference? One shuts down, the other builds up. Give them a role that matters: feeding the pet, setting the table, zipping their coat. Let them feel their contribution counts.

39

Celebrate effort, not only end results.

Praising only the results teaches performance. Celebrating effort grows resilience. It's not about what they achieve, it's how they engage. If we only celebrate success, children learn to fear failure. But when we highlight effort, they learn that taking action is worthy. Catch them mid-process. Offer, "I see how focused you are," or "You're working hard on that." Let them feel seen for showing up and normalize the learning journey.

Growth mindset starts in early years.

Growth mindset begins with how we respond to challenge. Children internalize what we say—especially about ourselves. "I'm not good at this" becomes their inner voice, unless we show them another way. Language is everything. They learn whether to give up or get curious based on what we model. Swap "I can't" with "How can I?"—especially out loud. Let your child hear you practice this shift in real-time. They'll borrow your mindset.

Play Is Your Child's Best Teacher

41

Play teaches everything worksheets cannot replace.

Play isn't a break from learning—it *is* the learning. It's your child's native language. While adults chase outcomes, children chase curiosity. That's where the real education lives. They learn communication, problem-solving, resilience, and joy. No worksheet can replicate the complexity of pretend play and exploring a variety of materials. Resist the urge to interrupt. Let play unfold naturally. Say less, observe more, and trust that what looks simple is actually profound.

Learning happens best through joyful play.

Joy is a neurological glue. When learning feels like play, the brain lights up. Joy increases attention, lowers stress, and deepens understanding. Serious doesn't equal effective. When children are relaxed, curious, and engaged, their brains retain more, connect faster, and thrive longer. Joy isn't extra—it's essential. Turn something mundane into play today—sorting laundry by color, counting grapes, making up a rhyme while brushing teeth. Engage in laughter because learning follows laughter.

43

Sensory play builds focus and regulation.

Children are wired to move and explore. Sensory play helps integrate emotions, body awareness, and attention. Touch, movement, and messy exploration aren't "extras"—they're how young brains regulate and grow. Sensory play helps children center, ground, and focus better later. Offer a sensory bin: rice, water, shaving cream, dough, beans or textured toys. Let them lead. Watch their body calm and their focus sharpen while regulation emerges through repetition and rhythm.

Risky play strengthens courage and confidence.

Children need real-world risks to build inner resilience. Risky play is how they learn their edges—both physically and emotionally. Climbing, balancing, jumping—these aren't dangerous indulgences, they're courage training. Risky play teaches children to assess, adapt, and trust themselves in real time. Resist the urge to say, "Be careful." Instead, ask: "Do you feel steady?" Support awareness, not fear. Watch your child's confidence grow when they sense you trust in their instincts.

45

Outdoor daily movement matters for learning.

Nature is the original classroom. Movement primes the brain for focus and learning. A stick becomes a wand; a tree becomes a story. Children weren't built for indoor stillness. Movement + nature regulate the nervous system, awaken the senses, and support lifelong learning. Offer plenty of outdoor time daily and let them lead. Follow the leaf, the bug, the puddle. Nature helps anchor the body and brain for the day ahead.

Creative play builds empathy and creativity.

During creative play, children experiment with new roles and explore how others think and feel. It's the earliest form of empathy and imagination in action. When your child becomes a dragon or a doctor, they're practicing perspective-taking, storytelling, and problem-solving. Pretend play builds brains and hearts. Instead of steering the story, join it. Ask, "Who should I be?" and let them lead. You're not teaching, you're connecting.

47

Let them explore, don't over-direct.

Exploration is how your child learns what matters to them. Over-direction and too much instruction hijack curiosity while turning play into performance. Backing off a little gives them the gift of discovery. Let boredom show up—it's often the gateway to deeper exploration. Bite your tongue during play today. Let silence lead. Watch where they go when no one is shaping the outcome.

Unstructured time fosters deep thinking skills.

Downtime is fertile ground for imagination. Without constant structure, children learn to solve problems, create meaning, and self-direct. It's not wasted time—it's essential. When children are constantly entertained, they lose the skill of directing their own focus. Unstructured time strengthens creativity, patience, and executive function. Block 30 minutes of unscheduled time today. No agenda. No task. Let them lead the way and see what emerges.

49

Less toys, more imagination, richer play.

Simplicity invites imagination. The fewer the toys, the more your child's brain does the work and creativity expands. Too many toys can clutter focus. Children need space to imagine. Cardboard boxes beat battery-operated anything, every time. Rotate toys weekly. Store some out of sight. Fewer choices = deeper play. It's intentional design. Keep only the items that spark open-ended play. Watch their creativity expand in the space you create.

Play builds social, emotional, cognitive skills.

Play is rehearsal for life. Every turn taken, story shared, or tower rebuilt is wiring your child for emotional and social success. In play, children practice negotiation, patience, empathy, persistence, and planning—all without knowing it. It's a developmental goldmine wrapped in joy. Watch your child play with others. Instead of intervening too soon, observe. Notice what they're learning—then support the repair if needed.

Words Create and Shape Their World

51

Words matter, they become inner scripts.

Language doesn't only describe reality—it creates it. Every word you speak becomes part of your child's inner library. What they hear from you now is what they'll say to themselves later. Speak as if you're writing their future self-talk. Reflect on what you say most often. Ask: "Would I want my child saying this to themselves?" If not, rewrite it. Choose a phrase you want your child to internalize; say it daily.

Speak kindly now; echoes last forever.

Kindness isn't fluff—it's foundational. A calm tone, gentle correction, or thoughtful response softens the moment and it echoes in your child's heart for decades. What you say in a rush may be remembered in slow motion. Kindness in the moment can become their anchor later. Be intentional with your language. Instead of "Hurry up!" offer, "We've got a few minutes—let's do this together."

53

Criticism wounds; encouragement fuels lifelong growth.

Children don't need to be made aware of their flaws. Encouragement allows for growth. It sees effort and intention. Criticism shrinks. Encouragement expands. A single critical comment can echo for years, while authentic encouragement builds resilience. Shift from flaw-finding to strength-spotting. "You're really good at noticing details," instead of "Why can't you focus?"

Narrate struggles; model problem-solving language.

Children often internalize only the outcome of a struggle unless we narrate the process. When you talk through your challenges aloud, you give children a script for handling hard things. Talk them through how you're figuring something out, not only when you're done. They borrow your language until they build their own. "I'm feeling frustrated. I think I'll take a breath and start again." Let them witness the process.

55

Sorry means repair, not only regret.

True apologies don't come from shame—they come from empathy. Sorry means more when it's paired with responsibility and repair. Teaching repair means helping your child feel the impact of their actions, then reconnect with care. After a misstep, guide your child with, "What can I do to make it right?" Repair is a skill—not a script. Model repair yourself. "You didn't deserve me taking frustration out on you. I'm sorry."

Speak how you want them speaking.

Children don't learn respectful language by being told—they learn by being shown. Your tone becomes their tone. The way you speak to them is how they'll speak to others and themselves. The way you handle hard moments teaches them how to speak under stress. Modeling respectful communication is the long game. Pick one area where tension usually rises (bedtime, transitions). Practice using the tone you want them to use.

57

Label strengths; they'll trust in themselves.

What you reflect becomes part of their self-image. When you name what's working, your child begins to see it too. Labeling strengths forms a perspective grounded in capability and growth. Strength-spotting helps children internalize who they are beyond behavior: thoughtful, patient, or persistent. Let a strength-based reflection be the last thing they hear at bedtime: "You noticed something really important and stayed focused." Name a strength with specificity.

"You're learning;" better than "Stop failing."

The way we respond to missteps matters. Correcting without connection can feel like criticism to children (and adults). "You're learning" reframes the behavior as growth and keeps the door open. "Stop that" or "Again?" often closes it with shame. When your child struggles, offer: "This is new. Learning takes practice." Let effort feel natural, not embarrassing. Language like that builds momentum, not shutdown.

59

Replace "Be good" with "Make choices."

"Be good" is vague, moralizing and centers approval. "Make kind choices" or "Notice what your body needs" shifts the focus to awareness and agency. This shift builds values-based behavior rather than performative obedience. Before a transition or social event, preview with: "What kind of choices do you want to make?" Empower self-direction over compliance. Use words that guide, not judge: "Be thoughtful. Be generous. Be yourself."

Your words shape lifelong self-trust.

Self-trust doesn't happen by accident—it's shaped in daily moments where our words affirm their instincts. Build the muscle of "I can trust myself." The way you speak today becomes your child's inner compass tomorrow. Language either invites them to trust themselves—or doubt. Speak in a way that builds self-trust. Pause before offering advice. Ask, "What feels right to you?" Honor their inner voice before layering on your own.

Raising Resilient, Adaptable, Strong Little Humans

61

Resilience grows from connected, secure relationships.

Children don't build resilience by being pushed—they build it by being held. When they trust you're there, they feel brave enough to attempt, fall, and get up again. You are the foundation they rise from. Secure relationships provide the support to move through it. In a hard moment, say, "I'm right here. We'll figure this out together." Courage first, challenge second. Resilience grows from connection: eye contact, loving touch, and soft voice.

Teach flexibility, life rarely goes perfectly.

Life is full of curveballs. Children learn to bend, not break, when we model adaptability. Flexibility isn't something you explain, it's something you practice together. It doesn't mean avoiding structure, it means showing how to flow with it. How you respond to change becomes their script for it. When plans shift, model a reframe: "That's not what we expected... let's see what else we could do." Invite possibility over panic.

63

Let them struggle; offer loving support.

Growth and struggle are twins. If we smooth the path too much, children lose the opportunity to build their strength. Struggle isn't failure—it's the work of growth. Don't rush to rescue. Sit beside the discomfort and let your presence be the soft landing. Stay close, not controlling. When your child gets stuck, resist jumping in. Ask, "Does this part feel tricky? Want to talk through it together?" Ask before telling.

Normalize challenges; growth comes through commitment.

Children grow more when challenges are accepted than when perfection is expected. Commitment to keep going matters more than always getting it "right." Challenges aren't shameful—they're part of mastery. Normalize them early so your child sees them as steps toward understanding. When they face a challenge, stay steady. Offer: "Challenges help us grow. You're still learning, and that's okay." Share a challenge you had that day. Normalize the learning loop out loud.

65

Comfort first, then problem-solve together.

Children need co-regulation before they can co-create solutions. Comfort makes them feel brave enough to reflect and do it again. A dysregulated brain is unable to problem-solve. Comfort doesn't coddle—it calibrates the nervous system. Soothe first. Then shift to what needs solving. Offer a "connection-first" response: hug, sit near, or hold their hand. Then move to curiosity: "What do you think we could do next time?"

Teach frustration tolerance through everyday moments.

Frustration isn't a problem to avoid—it's a skill to build. Every tough moment is a chance to stretch your child's window of tolerance, gently and consistently. Support doesn't mean fixing. It means staying near while they feel it. Let them wrestle with a puzzle, shoe, or story. If it feels hard, name it: "It seems frustrating and you're figuring it out." Let them know that the feeling and effort is great.

67

Weather disappointments together, don't rescue instantly.

Disappointment is inevitable. What matters is whether your child feels alone in it or supported through it. Don't rush to remove it. When we rescue too quickly, we rob children of resilience. When we stay close through disappointment, we teach emotional endurance and trust. When something doesn't go their way, sit next to the emotion. Offer: "That is disappointing. I'm here with you." No distraction. Presence.

Model optimism. Challenges create new possibilities.

Children learn optimism by watching how we hold disappointment. Show them that challenge doesn't close doors—it opens new ones. Optimism doesn't mean pretending things are easy, it means trusting we'll grow through them. When you model hope, you plant it. Reframe a recent challenge aloud: "That was tough, and I learned something new." Let them hear how you move forward without bypassing the hard.

69

Strength isn't toughness, it's inner adaptability.

True strength isn't about pushing through—it's about adjusting, reflecting, and choosing again. Children become strong when we honor their flexibility and their grit. Resilience is softening without collapsing. When we teach adaptability, we raise children who bend with life instead of breaking under it. Celebrate when your child adapts: "You switched gears so well when plans changed." Let strength mean fluidity, not force.

Let them fall, teach getting up.

Protecting your child from every fall protects them from growth, too. Let them stumble in small ways now so they build the muscles to rise later. Falling is part of the story. When they experience it, show them how to rise with support and self-trust. Don't rush to say, "You're okay." Offer: "What do you want to do next?" Help them see the fall as part of the process.

Sleep, Nutrition and Movement Support Growth

71

Well-rested children behave, learn better.

Sleep isn't a luxury—it's foundational. Many "behavior issues" are sleep-deprivation symptoms. Tired brains can't regulate. Prioritizing rest can shift everything. A rested brain processes emotions, makes better choices, and absorbs learning more easily. Exhaustion often looks like misbehavior. Notice and track patterns: does your child melt down more when tired? Create a bedtime buffer: 30 to minutes of low light, no screens, and soothing activities to signal "winding down."

Sleep routines shape lifelong health habits.

Bedtime doesn't have to be rigid—but it does need rhythm. Rhythm creates security. Predictable bedtime routines help the brain unwind and set the stage for deeper, more restorative sleep for years to come. Consistency helps the nervous system recognize when to power down. Anchor your evenings with a phrase: "It's time for us to slow down." Say it nightly as the first cue toward sleep. Rhythm becomes regulation.

73

Food battles aren't worth the fight.

Control at the table creates stress—for everyone. Pressure disrupts appetite and connection. Trust them to eat what they need, within the choices you offer. Forcing food teaches disconnection from internal cues. Mealtimes are about nourishment and relationship. Focus on the experience, not the bites. Drop the power struggle. Serve what you've planned, let them choose what to eat, and end the meal without commentary.

Offer variety, but trust their hunger.

Children eat what they need over time. Offering variety supports health; trusting their appetite supports autonomy. Both matter. You're the provider. They're the decider. Offering healthy options without pressure honors your child's natural hunger cues and builds body trust. Serve meals with one to two familiar foods and one new option. Trust them to explore in their own time.

75

Sugar spikes moods, real food nourishes.

Big mood swings can be traced to blood sugar spikes which does hijack emotions. Blood sugar crashes look a lot like tantrums. Real food steadies the nervous system. Simple, balanced meals help regulate emotions before behavior even begins. Observe your child's energy after meals. Add protein and fiber where possible to soften sugar's impact. Keep snacks simple: fruit + fat or carb + protein.

Balance blood sugar, prevent meltdowns early.

Meltdowns aren't always emotional—they're often biochemical. Stable blood sugar reduces reactivity and boosts focus. The brain needs even fuel to function. Before you assume "bad behavior," check for a blood sugar crash. The right fuel at the right time can prevent a spiral. Prevent crashes instead of reacting to them.Pack a protein-rich snack in the car or bag. Use it as a reset before transitions or after school.

77

Movement fuels brain growth and focus.

Children move because their brains are developing, not because they want to be wild. Movement wires learning and is a catalyst. Little bodies need to move to think and focus. Physical activity builds the brain's executive function and emotional regulation. Stillness comes after movement. Prioritize outside time before anything requiring attention. Nature + movement = brain power.

Sleep deprivation often mimics ADHD symptoms.

A tired brain struggles with focus and flexibility. Sleep deprivation can look like bad behavior when it's actually exhaustion. Lack of sleep can look like hyperactivity, distractibility, or even defiance. Before labeling behavior, check sleep patterns. Fatigue wears many disguises. Put your child to bed 20 minutes earlier for a week. Journal your child's behavior for a few days alongside their sleep totals. Patterns will show you where to focus first.

79

Active bodies support calm, focused minds.

Stillness isn't the goal—regulated stillness is. Movement helps the body process energy, emotions, and stress so the mind can engage with calm. The more movement a child gets, the easier it is to sit, focus, and listen later. Motion now means attention later. Build in one movement ritual daily—morning stretches, post-nap dance party, or an after-dinner walk. Use movement as a transition tool: Ten jumping jacks before quiet time.

Hydrated children handle emotions more easily.

Dehydration messes with mood, focus, and energy. Similar to adults, children crash faster when they're not properly hydrated. Tiny bodies lose water fast—and with it, patience and focus. Regular hydration keeps the brain and body steady. Water is regulation in a cup. Keep a child-size water bottle within reach throughout the day. Invite them to sip often—especially before and after transitions.

Social Skills are Learned through Experience

81

Teach kindness through your daily actions

Kindness isn't a concept—it's a way of being. Children learn kindness by how we treat them and others. Every interaction becomes part of their social blueprint. When you consistently treat your child with respect, they absorb it as natural. Let them witness compassion in motion. Model acts of kindness throughout your day.

Show empathy, they'll mirror it back.

Empathy is caught, not taught. When you empathize with your child's small struggles, you wire their brain for compassion. Your child learns how to care by being cared for. The more they feel seen, the more naturally they'll show up for others. When your child is upset, reflect what you see: "That really hurt your feelings, didn't it?" Stay with the feeling, not the fix.

83

Guide connection over giving up possessions.

Empathy isn't about handing things over—it's about noticing others. Teaching children to tune into how someone else feels fosters deeper connection than forced sharing ever could. We don't need to force generosity to build empathy. Instead of demanding a toy be shared, invite your child to notice how others feel. When your child is playing and another child shows interest, ask: "Can you tell what your friend might be feeling?" Stay curious.

Friendships need guidance, not forced sharing.

Real friendships take time, trust, and tools. Teaching consent in sharing builds true social awareness, not performative politeness. Forcing a child to share teaches that their boundaries don't matter. But guiding them toward kindness with consent lays the groundwork for healthy relationships. Offer: "When you're finished, let your friend know." Respect teaches boundaries and builds trust. Then sharing becomes a choice, not control.

85

Conflict resolution starts with feeling understood.

Jumping straight to solutions skips over emotion. When both children feel heard, they're more willing to collaborate, not compete. Before children can solve a conflict, they need to feel heard. Understanding comes before resolution. Skip this step, and the conflict will recycle. "Let's take turns telling what happened. I'll listen to each of you." Then allow them to come up with a solution together with your guidance.

Name the feeling, not the fault

When children name a feeling instead of assigning blame, they stay connected and understood. “I felt left out” opens doors—“You never include me!” slams them. Help your child tune into their emotional experience, not only the behavior around it. You can guide by modeling: “I felt frustrated, not mad *at you*—I’m overwhelmed.”

87

Problem-solving grows from small disagreements first.

Early conflict is healthy—if handled well. It gives children a chance to learn negotiation, compromise, and boundary-setting from the inside out. Disagreements are practice grounds for future relationships. When children learn to navigate small conflicts with support, they gain confidence for bigger ones. When conflict arises, don't rush in. Sit nearby and say, "Sounds like you're working on figuring this out. Want help or space?"

Let them express; don't dismiss feelings.

Feelings aren't problems to fix. They're data. When we rush past them, children learn to hide them. When we stay present, they learn to trust them. When you allow feelings without judgment, you teach emotional fluency. Dismissing them may calm the surface, but it creates confusion inside. When your child expresses emotion, offer: "That makes sense." No fixing. No redirecting. Only a pause for presence. Let it be enough.

89

Emotional intelligence shapes future life success.

IQ might get the spotlight, but EQ builds the foundation. Children who can name, regulate, and relate grow into adults who lead with empathy and adapt with resilience. The ability to navigate emotions shapes relationships, careers, and confidence more than academics ever could. Begin each day with a quick emotional check-in: "How are you feeling in your body?" Normalize emotional self-awareness as a daily rhythm.

Teach respect, but demand none mindlessly.

Respect is mutual and relational awareness, not obedience or a one-way street. Teaching it requires modeling it. Demanding it without offering it creates fear, not connection. When it's forced, it turns performative. When children feel respected, they naturally reflect it. Model it before you expect it. Shift from "Be respectful" to "Let's show each other kindness." Explain what respect looks like in action.

Be Present. This Stage Goes Fast

91

Childhood is short, presence matters most.

They won't remember every detail—but they'll remember how it felt to be with you. Presence builds memory, connection, and security. There's no rewind button. This season, with all its chaos and beauty, is fleeting. Presence doesn't mean constant attention—it means attuned attention. Choose one part of your day—bedtime, bath, or breakfast—and put your phone down. Be all in; Let them feel your availability in a way that sticks.

Your energy sets the home tone.

You're the emotional thermostat. Your energy—not your words—sets the climate. When you slow down, soften, or reset, the room shifts too. Children absorb energy faster than instructions. Regulated presence creates secure space and dysregulation spreads. You lead with how you are, not what you say. Before you enter a high-stress moment, take a grounding breath. Ask yourself: "What energy do I want to bring in?"

93

Slow down, notice, enjoy small moments.

Joy often hides in the ordinary. Slowing down gives you access to the sweetness that rushing steals. It's in their laugh. Their play. That one weird question. You don't need more time—you need more noticing. Presence lives in the micro-moments, not only milestones. Choose one slow moment: brushing hair, playing blocks, walking to the car. Let it stretch. Notice what's there. End the day with one thing you want to remember.

Focus on connection, not constant correction.

Correction without connection builds resistance. But connection builds trust—and trust invites growth. The real teacher? Correct less. Connect more. Parenting from disconnection doesn't work. Connection opens the door to all the guidance you are offering. Before correcting, first ask: "Am I connected right now?" Pause for eye contact, touch, or play before guiding. Then ask: "Do you need a hug or a break?" Meet the need behind the behavior.

95

Your wellbeing influences their emotional world.

Your nervous system is their blueprint. When you care for yourself, you give them permission to value their own inner world too. They don't need a perfect parent, only a present one. And presence requires you to have some internal fuel. Ask yourself daily: "What do I need to feel more like me?" Make the answer visible—your children are watching. Refilling you is part of parenting them.

Model self-care, they're always watching.

Self-care isn't selfish. Your children learn how to value themselves by watching how you treat yourself. You're showing them what adulthood looks like. Boundaries, rest, and joy all model worth—a version they won't need to recover from. Invite them into your rhythm: "I'm going to take a quiet moment so I can feel good in my body." Build in shared quiet and let them hear you choose yourself.

97

Overwhelm less, simplify childhood for them.

A full calendar doesn't equal a full childhood. Children thrive in rhythm, not rush. When you simplify, you help them settle. Too many choices, toys, or transitions can crowd their nervous systems. Simplicity is a gift—it creates space for presence, imagination, and peace. Declutter one space or schedule block. More white space = more room for connection, curiosity, and calm.

Savor this stage; time moves fast.

There will be a last time you pick them up, tie their shoes, or hear that silly mis-pronunciation. Don't miss it while waiting for "later." You're living the days you'll miss. Even the exhausting ones. Savoring isn't about loving every minute—it's about noticing the moments you'll never get back. Each night, whisper one thing you loved about the day. Let it anchor the memory—for both of you.

99

Trust yourself, parent with love first.

There's no one right way. The more you trust your intuition and values, the clearer everything else becomes. Your love is the map. You don't need every answer—you need alignment. Parenting from love, not fear, anchors your presence and your choices. Write down your top three parenting values. When unsure, ask: "Which of these does this decision support?"

Connection over control, always choose presence.

Behavior doesn't change through control—it changes through relationship. Connection invites cooperation in a way correction never will. Control is tempting—but connection is transformative. Choose the relationship, even when it's messy. That's where trust lives. That's where real influence begins. End your day with repair: "I may have been tense today. I'm still learning too. I love being your parent."

Acknowledgments

This book was not written alone.

I live through the lens that we are never the same person from one moment to the next. Every interaction—whether fleeting or profound—shapes us. From the mundane, like a coffee drive-through or a quick hello to the mail carrier, to life-altering experiences like buying a home or sitting in an urgent care waiting room—each exchange carries energy. Whether or not we're aware of it, we're absorbing and offering something. Even the spaces we inhabit—homes, rooms, buildings—hold echoes of those who came before us. We're always becoming.

Because we are always becoming, this book is not only a collection of insights—it's a living, breathing tribute to transformation. To the invisible exchanges, the quiet reckonings, and the unseen moments that shape who we are.

This work is a mosaic of every encounter that left an imprint—those who challenged me, held me, walked away, or walked beside me. Each offered something sacred.

May these pages feel like a pause, a mirror, and a gentle nudge toward tuning into the energy all around you—and within you.

To the families and parents, I've worked with over the years—you've shaped every word on these pages. Your vulnerability, your curiosity, and your love for your children inspired this work more than you know. You've helped me shape this language into something real.

To Claudia, the architect of everyday magic at The Cove School—thank you for continuing to bring this vision to life each day with presence, heart, and unwavering dedication. Your deep connection with children, steady leadership with staff, and ability to hold the pulse of our work allow this vision to grow in ways both intentional and alive. There are no words to express my appreciation. I'm deeply grateful for your partnership and the wisdom you bring to it all.

To the children—both mine and yours—thank you for reminding me what matters: wonder, presence, truth, love and essence. You are the teachers we don't always remember to learn from.

To my mentors and teachers—your wisdom, patience, and presence reminded me what it means to hold space and how to hold space for others.

To my clients and communities across **The Cove School**, **With Pause** and **Trusting Equus**—thank you for showing me that healing isn't about changing who we are, but about returning to what's always been true. Sometimes it looks like sitting in the barn, listening, and being still enough to hear the wisdom beneath the noise.

To my parents, Vickie and Danny—for bringing me into this world and your unconditional love and support. Your journey planted the seeds for mine.

To my brother Brian—thank you for holding your piece of our story.

To Rusty—thank you for standing and walking next to me in the mess, the growth, and the becoming.

And to Noah, Cain, and Selah—there are no words big enough. You're the reason I began listening more closely, slowing down more often, and choosing respect and connection even when it was hard. Thank you for being the "why" behind all my becoming.

To my horses—Genie, Stella, Po, and Baker—thank you for being the wisest co-regulators and clearest mirrors I've ever known. You bring people back to themselves in ways no language can.

To the reader holding this book—whether in a season of chaos or calm—I hope these words give you permission to slow down, see clearly, and trust yourself. You're not here to get it perfect. You're here to be present. And that changes everything. You are seen. You are sacred. You are never alone in this.

May this book meet you exactly where you are—and walk with you as you are becoming.

Closing Note

If you've made it to this page, you've already done something powerful: You paused. You reflected. You showed up with curiosity instead of certainty.

If there's one truth I return to again and again, it's this: Our children are not ours to control and don't need shaping. They need space.

They came into this world with their own frequency, their own path, their own truth. They don't need fixing. They need *us*—regulated, connected, and tuned in.

The greatest gift we can offer is to see them clearly, trust their unfolding, and **get out of their way.**

This doesn't mean stepping back. It means **showing up with presence** instead of pressure—modeling the wholeness we want them to remember in themselves, and allowing them to feel free to be exactly who they already are.

This work isn't about being more—it's about becoming *more you.* And the more you trust yourself, the more your children learn to trust themselves too.

Keep coming back to the small moments. That's where the magic lives.

This book was never meant to give you all the answers. If it helped you loosen the grip, tune into your own wisdom, and lead with love instead of fear—then it did what it was meant to.

I hope that these pages reminded you of your strength, softened some edges, and helped you trust your path a little more. Whether you're feeling inspired, exhausted, uncertain, or all of the above—You're in it.

You're not only raising a child. **You're transforming a future**—and remembering your own essence along the way.

Thank you for letting me walk beside you.

It's been an honor.

With deep trust and gratitude,
Renee

About the Six-Word Lessons Series

Legend has it that Ernest Hemingway was challenged to write a story using only six words. He responded with the story, “For sale: baby shoes, never worn.” The story tickles the imagination. Why were the shoes never worn? The answers are left up to the reader’s imagination.

This style of writing has a number of aliases: postcard fiction, flash fiction, and micro-fiction. Lonnie Pacelli was introduced to this concept in 2009 by a friend, and started thinking about how this extreme brevity could apply to today’s communication culture of text messages, tweets and Facebook posts. He wrote the first book, *Six-Word Lessons for Project Managers*, then he and his wife Patty started helping other authors write and publish their own books in the series.

The books all have six-word chapters with six-word lesson titles, each followed by a one-page description. They can be written by entrepreneurs who want to promote their businesses, or anyone with a message to share.

See the entire ***Six-Word Lessons Series***
at **6wordlessons.com**

www.ingramcontent.com/pod-product-compliance
Lightning Source LLC
Chambersburg PA
CBHW070642050426
42451CB00008B/269
* 9 7 8 1 9 6 7 2 5 6 0 2 0 *